BEDTIME

Clare Pollard

bedtime

BLOODAXE BOOKS

ISBN: 1 85224 593 X

First published 2002 by
Bloodaxe Books Ltd,
Highgreen,
Tarset,
Northumberland NE48 1RP.

www.bloodaxebooks.com
For further information about Bloodaxe titles
please visit our website or write to
the above address for a catalogue.

Bloodaxe Books Ltd acknowledges
the financial assistance of Northern Arts.

Cover printing by J. Thomson Colour Printers Ltd, Glasgow.

Printed in Great Britain by
Cromwell Press Ltd, Trowbridge, Wiltshire.

To Richard

Contents

9   Fears of a Hypochondriac Insomniac
11   The Crimes of Love
12   The Bunker in Berlin
13   Buying Manhattan
14   Tourism
15   Hallelujah
16   Character-shaping Childhood Experience
17   Hometown
18   Thinking of England
22   Conspiracy Theory
23   Chick's Flick
24   A Greek Morning
25   Dark Lady
27   The Smear Test
28   Knowledge
30   Confessional Piece
31   Madder
33   Adventures with Lola
35   My Bed
38   Puppetry
39   Posing for Dante Gabriel Rossetti
40   A Winter's Tale
41   The Black Widow
42   Doubter's Sonnets
45   Bed Scenes
47   And Desire Shall Fail
48   Fantasy Dinner Party
50   Knowing Our Limits
51   Letter from a Father
54   On Tragic Pleasure
56   Work and Lunch
58   Post-
59   The Florist's
60   Morning
61   Gender Wars
62   Oistros
63   To Undefine
64   And Another Bloody Thing...

Fears of a Hypochondriac Insomniac

I know the poetry of sickness –
ailment to zymosis,
and recall it, feverish, in blinded dark,
awake again: the alarm claiming 3:14
in figures neon as blood on a light-box,
your heart's *slump*, *slump* thrumming near my bent ear,
the window open to ambulance sirens and possible screams.

Can I hear your breath? Or is that the trick of gas
whispering through slender copper pipes?
Your guts gurgle like a radiator, your heart
scares me, with its stop, start.
The opacity of our bodies alarms me, their capacity for lies
          and secrets:
marrow gammy as old spunk in the femur,
histamines threatening hissy fits beneath our skin,

wrong signals crackling through acetylchline,
aneurysms, ulcers,
the arteries thickening like moss-plush gutters.
The lung my hand is pressed above
could catch a darkness, like the shadow of a hawk
above a furrowed field of harvest mice.
A clot, like an inky full-stop, could nudge up to the heart.

Your body jerks a jolt, slams up
like some mad professor's monstrous creation
electrified alive by storm-light –
my mouth crawls needily near your ear:
'Are you all right? Are you okay?'
Yes, you say,
it was just one of those dreams where you fall.

And I know we have it all,
that elsewhere in this town loved ones are stretched out on stretchers,
in corridors, with clean floors that smell of swimming pools,
steadying themselves on eyefuls
of white walls and Magritte prints,
and waiting for one of the not-enough-beds
with fear they have a right to.

And I know my life is perfect, or near perfect,
that anything better is a beautiful dream –
like God, or The One – but no more.
I have writing, you, my health –
so why this wakefulness: insomnia
diseased with hypochondria,
these morbid X-rays I imagine of your sleep-slowed body?

It is luck's fault, for giving you to me,
for all this bounty, fluke and preciousness.
For leaving me nothing to long for but this, *now*, for longer.
Bodies we love must always be taken,
and at night I wait for the signs I don't want,
hooked round your body, its mess of cartilage and capillary,
a very human shield.

Where your bone skims the skin,
at clavicle, hip and heel,
and where veins thread at your wrists, brow and penis –
these places provoke suffocating grief, for what I'll lose.
Last week, you confessed you had been scared shitless
that some humdrum ache was actually cancerous.
My mortal love, what fucking fools we are.

The Crimes of Love

You may count on me as on a second self
RENÉE-PELAGIE DE SADE,
writing to her husband in prison

Beloved Donatien, that *vous* you wrote
adds to your list of horrors. Pen *pet*, inscribe *Dear friend*,
ink out *I love you still.*
Your mistress, Nature,
abhors a vacuum; I, this orange bedroom, my winter one,
without your scenes.
I am staring at the tortoise-shell clock.
The tric-trac table, tapestries and chandeliers are props,
with no direction.

I enclose: ointment for you-know-what; beef marrow,
eel pâté, cherries. A thrush.
That flask you asked for, sadly, could not be found –
no neck fits your specified dimensions.

I embrace you and suffer greatly,
                                        Renée-Pelagie.

PS, so you have guessed I'd use invisible ink too –
lemon's juices, tart as our pleasures were.
The mantelpiece still bears the nicks of your tally;
my thighs are still woven with the snags of your knife.
Nothing feels, not like you, please write more: write
of boiled-oil douches, desecration, hung whores.
Your description of hot tongs on mons veneris made me panting-faint.
I am your second self;
                    you cover mastery, I'll cover self-restraint.

The Bunker in Berlin

Let Rome in Tiber melt, and the wide arch
Of the ranged empire fall. Here is my space.
        SHAKESPEARE,
        Anthony and Cleopatra

Auschwitz and Dresden are words, that's all.
Because of your love, this room is everywhere.
Our flame paints the walls shifting gold, like my pure
German hair, which you love. Candle-fat dribbles
tears, opaque as pus. What power you've left

secured champagne, bone-dry. It goes right to my head –
you have some too, now you're no longer needing
to preserve control; are past that.
The home-movies I filmed show you relaxed, your shirt
unbuttoned in the sun. Blondi, your Aryan hound

nuzzled at your hand: stripped pine pale, loved –
though you would whip it when you had to –
and then, later, fucking. You fucked with a brute heart,
fists clenched – fighting yourself. Dick up to the hilt
in my conquered cunt. Your Europe. Your reclaimed land.

Twice I've tried to end myself. Don't think I haven't heard
of ovens, and showers, and Lodz, where soldiers
dropped babies like sandbags on their bayonets –
but what's a pulped heap of sick-sweet syruping bodies
when I'm pressed by your body – hard and Tyrol-snow white?

This is life. Tomorrow's death. We've cyanide
and pistols, they'll not find us waiting here
to be their freaks, their puppets, but nobly dead –
wed with a ring melted down from Jewish teeth;
my pact, mein Führer, with whatever you are.

12

Buying Manhattan
(New York, December 2000)

It's 2-for-1 (or B.O.G.O.F.) at *McDonalds* in New York,
New York, but billboards bully me to swap my greenbacks
(which smell dirty) for other national treats: seasonal lattes –
eggnog or gingerbread – cheeseburger Wednesdays, then special
brunch deals: grits, pancakes with bacon and maple
syrup that looks like what they dredge from smokers' lungs
in anti-smoking campaigns, apple pie like mom made,

bagels with lox from the diner in *When Harry Met Sally* (where
she fakes it). The streets advertise nasally, with wafts of chai
and mocha, and pockets of the smell of roasting nuts.
Status-symbol shorthaired dogs (apartment friendly!) yap
at hot-dogs; dispensers sneeze mustard out like snot.
I pass *Gap*, *Starbucks* – the street panting steamy breath
up my skirt – *Niketown*, *Borders*. My hands, which, defensively,

clamp on my handbag, are cramped with indecision –
I need a sign: SHOP / DON'T SHOP.
When we were landing, sound clotted to a hum as the plane
plunged. America drifted below banks of cloud:
phosphorescence on a dark ocean, delicate fish-spines of light.
And then the startling grid: urban chaos contained
in mathematics; a city mapping itself. New York,

New York! On the ground order's less visible.
The skaters by the Rockefeller Center flip and clunk, and bruise
their bums, and beggars beg outside *The Body Shop*, bundled up
in cast-offs and headlines. *I'm the Prez says Dubya.*
I wind up buying a large apple donut in *Dunkin' Donuts*.
The sweetness sets my teeth on edge,
but still, it tastes good – being a part of it.

Tourism

Spain was gold as saffron, and Borolo red,
a fat moon in the sky, and *sangría*-soaked head.
Sitting at wooden bars and ordering *jamón*,
blood-sausage, the terrible violence of the sun

as it mapped tender countries out onto my back,
and curtains drawn at noon in the room where we'd fuck.
Then the bullfight, the beast's wide neck wholly pierced through,
it spinning in madness's labyrinth as though

on heat, the strutting matador's cape draped before
its stagger, luring its fierce weight to the dust floor.
Quietened, I drank warm *Cruz Campos*, took photos,
soberly watched the corpse dragged off, and clapped, and rose.

But these memories only return to me as willed –
it is your face, your touch, that floods back though uncalled:
you splayed out, feverish and sleepy in the shade,
or racing over burning sand; how you tasted

when our daily picnic of bread and *chorizo*
spiced up your tongue, or how when on the pedalo
I threw up, you took my abuse all the way back.
The suntan and sucking mosquitoes left no mark,

but you did, you do, and the only trips I take
which matter are to get to you – those weekend breaks
next to your heart, and though I never will possess
the real you, and we will remain as foreigners

my use of love never translating into yours,
I can make do with the snapshots that I have stored:
thumb through them at night, in the darkness, when a sea
of silence rushes in to estrange you from me.

Hallelujah

Sand stretched out like the margin of a parchment.
My mouth was a wineskin, drained.
Dust clutched at my soles, as I paused to cool

in the door-frame's shadow,
in silent adoration of Mary – her fumbling grace.
She was beside the window, kneading,

her palm-leaf eyes still onion-wet –
a hymn beneath her breath.
It's hard to explain how it all... It was so sudden –

how the sun struck her tan cheek; soft, dark hairs stuck
to its film of sweat. Stumbling,
she cuffed the clay jug of milk

and whitened the room,
and took in a gasp of joy, on her knees now.
I make things from wood. Carved tongue fits exactly

into groove. That face was incandescent, perfect
with a beauty that I could only gape at:
could not work up with my hands.

The air in the line of her eyes held specks of dust, skin, her;
they blended and danced like stars in the shaft of light,
above the table that I had made.

Character-shaping Childhood Experience

It is funny, but not, the way the slightest slight,
the tiniest trinket, or token, or word left unsaid
can nudge a life off-course – a child's life,
for then the little things are disproportionate as your head,

and your self is pink jelly pouring into a mould –
bunny? mouse? conventional? –
if there's too much water, or you nick a cube to gnaw,
it won't set, or won't set right.

This isn't about blame, the who did what to who –
who had the cat you loved put down,
or believed *him*, or had you supperless; slapped.
Sometimes it's just the world acting upon you,

in its awful, allegorical, magical way.
I'm thinking of the time I got a helium balloon,
at the village fair, that seemed as other
as an astronaut's handbag, a fun-sized moon,

a pet cloud, someone else's thought bubble,
and I thought I was just it, cool, a 'dude' or something
until it flicked free of my flummoxed fingers, drifted
up from my poor reflexes; the desperate, pumping fist.

It was lost, always, off to 'heaven' irrecoverably
as Jenny's great uncle, or our budgie, that took off –
a squawk of feathers, a Red Indian's last stand –
through the front door, when Mary answered it to me,

and spiralled up into its big, blue death –
or more prosaically, towards budgie flu, and owls.
After that, I refused helium balloons.
They brought too great a burden of responsibility –

to know, if you let concentration slip for just a moment,
it is gone, always; always and entirely your fault.
I could never be a doctor after that, or play team games,
or keep a dog, or be the one who loved less.

Acknowledgements

Acknowledgements are due to the editors of the following publications in which some of these poems first appeared: *Dreamcatcher*, *Leviathan Quarterly*, *Magma*, *Poetry Review*, *Prop*, *Rising*, *The Reater*, *The Rialto* and *Words*.

Hometown

A place is what you make it, but though she tried
to make something safe, twist something to pine for
out of this place, its stopped fountain eyes
and broken glass smile, she just got made herself:
moulded into a stoop and engraved with apathy.

Nights out aren't what they used to be.
People have moved on, so just a quiet one tonight –
no glitter, sick or tongues like fingers down her throat –
just a pub full of F-ing and the blind;
drunken eyes shut off to debts and the dripping
for fear of going staring mad.

At school they wondered why she was depressed –
her wounds were dressed,
she came top in that English test.
So what if she was lonely, hated, numb?
in maths she came out best!
Blood comes out under the cold tap, snap out of it.

And through the years the town strung up her tears
in bitter fairy-lights down every street.
In clubs there are imprints of her knees beside toilets,
disco globes caked with last year's tears.
And the suicide rate has slid up again,
razors trying to be born beneath each paving slab, smashing
up the concrete with their eager silver beaks.

There is a whole history of hurt hangs over her,
a tarpaulin full of rain that is about to fall in.
All that stops her leaving is the thought that tomorrow
she can walk out of this place, and the pain too.

Thinking of England

And let the lesson be – to be yersel's,
Ye needna fash gin it's to be ocht else.
To be yersel's – and to mak' that worth bein'...
  HUGH MacDIARMID
  A Drunk Man Looks at a Thistle

Let me take you on a journey to a foreign land...
  WILLIAM HAGUE

I

Dusk-light; the news tells of another train derailed,
and shoppers buying up the shops, and livestock
being herded to the chop – their chops unfit to eat –
and politicians once more putting foot to mouth.
Through my east-end window –
                                        over the tangled tree,
the council houses: some sardined with children,
catering-sized gallon tubs of cooking oil empty beside their bins;
some sheltering one of the three million children still in poverty;
some sold to Thatcher's fortunate –
now worth hundreds of thousands, more,
with rents devised to make even the well-off poor –
over the kids and dogs on a hanky of grass,
the burnt-out car, the hush-hush trendy warehouse bar,
ISLAM UNITE scrawled on a wall –

a man's voice trails its skittering wail across the sky,
and all around me people are preparing to pray
to a God to whom I am one of the damned.

II

And what did our great-grandmothers taste?
Perhaps pie and mash and jellied eels, or hash, pease pudding,
cobbler, cottage pie,
                            pasties and pickled eggs.
when I was small there was still Spam and jellied ham –
semolina, parkin, treacle tart.

18

Why have we not stood with our mothers,
floured and flushed beside the oven door,
watching our first Yorkshire puddings:
how their globed bellies swell?
Why was this not passed daughter to daughter?
When did the passing stop?
When did we choose to steal instead
from the daughters of all those we have hated or hurt:
gnocchi, noodles, couscous, naan, falafel, jerk?
For dinner I have chicken dupiaza from a foil tray –
how fitting England's national dish is not homemade but takeaway.
Through thrift – the rent is due – I boil my own rice up,
long-grain American.

III

You're so fortunate, they would exclaim, as I took photographs
of them beside King's Chapel, or of willows washing
their hair in the Cam, *to have all of this history around you.*

England's history is medieval pogroms;
it is Elizabeth, her skin a crust of Dover-white,
loosing galleons to pillage fruits, tobacco, men.
The bulging-eyed thieves swinging to the crowd's delight
metres from Shakespeare's Globe;
                                        stripping the churches;
Becket bleeding buckets on the floor;
and work-houses for the poor,
and the slave-trade; and raping the wife –
lie back and think of… crinolines, Crimea.
Missionaries hacking their one true path through the jungle.
Winston swearing: *We will fight them on the beaches!*

These people held the cargo of my genes within their blood.
Not all were good.
                        But how can I be held up as accountable?
And yet, all of the good they earned, and blessed me with
brings with it blame. Today I filled a form in –
ticked *White British* with a cringe of shame.

I am educated, middle-class, housed, well.
I am fat and rich on history's hell.

IV

I remember bracken, and heather, and a gusty, gutsy
wind, and a plastic tub of windberries that filled
and emptied, its ink writing a whodunit on my face.

I remember Southport, where granny said fine ladies had once
gone to purchase linens, and the best. Catching the miniature
train down to Happy-Land, and my name in wet sand,

and my grandfather towelling the sand off my legs,
and then our picnic in the car – tinned salmon sandwiches,
a flask of tea, crosswords. A Penguin biscuit.

I remember sitting in an American bar having to squint
to read about abortion laws by the dim candlelight,
and sipping my six-dollar Cosmopolitan – with a dollar tip –

and thinking of our local; its open fire, the rain
on its windows, and you in it. Maybe on a Sunday
after a walk on the heath, and lamb with mint sauce,

and thinking how I never could leave.

V

Just finishing off the curry, when the football starts.
An England game. Satellites are readying themselves
to bounce the match around the globe,
and prove that we are not the power we were.

The crowd belts out 'God Save the Queen',
though they do not believe in God or Queen;
their strips red, white and blue –
two of these being borrowed hues; loaned colours we use
to drown out the white noise of ourselves.
We are the whitest of the white:
                                        once this meant *right* –
Christ's holy light; the opposite of night, or black –
but now it only points to lack, the blank of who we are.

Who ever celebrates St George's Day?
And did you hear the one about the Englishman...?

A friend of mine at home's a Bolton Wanderers fan:
they chant *White Army*.

VI

And then the news again, at ten –
sometimes it makes you want to pack and leave it all:

the floods, the fuel, the teacher shortage in the schools,
the bombing of Iraq, the heart attacks, long working hours
and little sex, racist police, cigarette tax, grants all axed,
three million children still in poverty,
the burnt out car, the takeaway,
the headlines about Krauts, the lager louts,
the wobbly bridge they built, the colonial guilt,
the needless pain, the rain, the rain,

the pogroms, the pink globe, the tangled tree,
the Raj, the rape, the linens,
all the endless fucking cups of tea...

but everyone speaks English now,

and sometimes, a voice trails its skittering wail across the sky,
and I feel not just gratitude, but pride.

Conspiracy Theory

Inside our local at one o'clock
    During a lock-
in, sinking enough pints to turn things starry,
    listening whilst Len tells me,
    the space landing's a sham –
the 'so-called' moon designed by man,

a magic-of-Hollywood mock-up,
    script a knock-up
by some hack; silver spray, cutting-edge lighting,
    Neil Armstrong dangling on strings –
    I open up some crisps,
and (slurringly) object to this.

'They wouldn't!' I protest. 'Why not?' he
    demands of me,
getting up to get another round in.
    'Think now – they'd save a billion.
    The hoped for cheesy end
is guaranteed if you pretend.'

And then it all comes clear – how Their plan,
    that step for man,
was one into this future of New Labour,
    Popstars, virtual war, PR,
    and – soon – Jurassic Park.
This spinning off into the dark.

Chick's Flick

Let's not pretend that, really, I can make us
into anything you want.
Even if I go out with my girlfriends twice a week,
and end phone calls first,
and never buy you gifts you wouldn't dream of buying me,
purely for the pleasure of your pleasure,
I will still have my lines.
They will still slip through the crack of my mouth,
that faultline of my face:
'Why didn't you ring me last night' –
'Stay longer' – 'You never say you love me any more.'

When was I handed this script?
Perhaps at five, as my Barbie doll, teetering
on permanent tiptoes, kissed Ken with her whole plastic body.
Perhaps at seven, when my breath crushed a flame
for the hope of five inky fingers clutching mine,
through playtime, and always.

And if I tore the script's pages, let it tremble
like skin, and then crack to a fist on the fire,
it would not help, for these words are what I am made of.
There is nothing about me of interest but the monstrous,
insatiable, stubborn scale of my love.
It has always been this way –
the half-joking struggle under sleep-warmed sheets, forced
lightness in the voice: 'Wilt thou be gone? It is not yet
near day: It was the nightingale and not the lark.'

It is a desperate act, this willing him needy; day dark.

A Greek Morning

As much as they hoped, there was no leprosy –
my body pulping to the symbol of the mind they say I have.
The tragedy was Troilus's, and I was denied
such catharsis; I simply awake by Diomede
daily, sucked bone-dry by wine and the absences,
cursing my illiterate heart.

He is in a sliding morning sleep,
his hirsute back bared like a boar's,
his fingers, their pads fleshy as dates, circling my rim.
I slip my skull from his arm-pit, realign myself with him,
and he murmurs Criseyde, a name I believe
means false in Troy.

Who am I if those seven letters are abstracted?
the name has slipped from my mind.
Must I spend my days in predictable deceits,
a breathing allegorical character?
When I cry out for Troilus in the night
is it truth I am wet for?

Last week, I am told, Troilus died with low laughter
on his lips, for the lust he expended on me,
died wishing the whole of his heart had been God's.

Diomede's sweat smears my skin
with its signature notes of thyme and garlic.
He yawns warmly, disturbed by his cock crowing;
I try to elide my breaths. My sweet Troilus,
I always knew that you would stop loving me,
and I pushed and I pushed until your love spiralled
from my wintered fingers like a dry leaf.
I always told myself your love was less than mine,
and it was true.

Dark Lady

To create, I've destroyed myself...I'm the empty stage where actors act out various plays.

FERNANDO PESSOA

That fall, I shouldered through market –
cidery-apple ferment, meat's funk smell –
past cripples lugging their own weight through faeces,
bastards, beggars, bargains,
chickens wrestling airlessly in a slow rain of quills,
rumoured witches, scurvy-unstitched sea adventurers,
and pushed into the thick of the Globe,
to catch a clutch of words,
a *tum-te-tum* to match my own quick pulse.

It struck me, how the stages jut of sheltering almost-sky –
with its violet crust, its stars thick as spittle –
made the real thing seem dull as an English puddle,
and I wanted a part of it, felt slack and dun
beside your narrow-hipped Rosalinds and Kates;
the fuzz on their bound and secret bodies.

Aftershow, I sought you out:
found you scribbling by scant fire,
the pads of your fingers Moorish, and your mouth
expressive, as we tupped against the tilted desk,
plashing the ink to the ground.
And I vowed myself your groundling, one back for your beast,
after that went each week
to watch the fools, feasts, fighting for honour –
the hundred stunted hearts you might have had.
Sometimes you would stand in the wings, in the margins
of yourself: deferential to clawing, thirsting, unstoppable will.
Your own self was so huge and still
it heaved in you like absence.

Then, later, we'd perform scenes in your tick-quivering bed.
My monster always made me find signs of your other lover –
bruises smudged on you in fervour, in the dips
down into her dripping, dark well.

I thought to make you feel for flesh as well,
my fingers tugging at you,
making you trace my gemmed rind, lap my ripe cut,
staging hate; my abhorrence all love.
But still you'd sup the wine
and quietly thank me for fourteen well-wrought lines,
and what you could have felt,
had you not wholly known my heart.

The Smear Test

It was nothing to worry about, for it was not
intimidating, but funny almost, the slurpy sounds
that flapped from her vagina as he cranked it open;
the modesty blanket, that veiled no one's view but hers,
as though she'd gag to see her sex exposed.
It was comedy, the way she had to splay
her thighs wide enough to welcome a rugby squad.

And it was nothing to worry about, for it was not
painful, but tender almost, the spatula nosing
into her tight hole like a coy mouse, an elfin penis,
a fork gently testing the haddock is cooked through.
No, it was nothing to worry about.

And if her boyfriend hadn't told her that later,
pissed as a cunt and weeping like a raped whore,
she had hit him and hit him and screamed: 'Fuck off
and don't touch me, don't ever fucking touch me,'
she would never have dwelt on it.

Knowledge

The Death of Innocence, the papers called it, though
they'd said that just a month ago,
                        and the guilty children played
computer games in the station. They'd killed her off the beaten track:
hedgerow, half-blown dandelions, rats –
and now the plane tree blossoms with grief's gifts –
soft toys which
              dangle, lynched, from branches thick with turning leaves.

Voice box cracked, a cloth-eared cat trembles in the wind,
whilst piglet's leg dawdles on a tendon thread, and a thread-bare bear
has lost its eye to birds.
                 Among the hairy roots mute creatures breed,
laid out for the dead girl as for a pharaoh's pleasure, after –
ciphers to disguise an innocence lost with innocence
as branded by the Disney corporation –
                    saccharine as antidote to aberration.

But the teddy's fur is salted, sodden, queasy green as moss –
Papa Smurf's shit splattered. These toys speak of death and rot,
the weak spots where a body splits.
                 They echo scenes from playroom tortures –
how you scalped your doll, then skewered her breasts with pens;
         thick, black blood
clotting – or how with paper scissors you sliced hissing wounds
         into plastic necks.
Perhaps, too, the boys who ended her just saw a doll –
no suffering self, but put-together limbs, a saw-dust heart
they poured out on the path –
                  an object made for their amusement.

You're playing in Heaven now, a note spells out beside the crackle-
         wrapped anemones.
It is a spidery hand, one forced by Mummy's wishes to well-
         meaning sentiment.

But play taps into darkness,
                        it reveals the evil latent in us all,
and these images of prelapsarian beasts will only bloat and burst
beneath the heaven's tears; the rain which beats the blooms
until they cannot help but hang their heads.

Confessional Piece

My post A-level summer was a sullen, sopping one.
Rain glazed the garden.
Mum folded and pressed hankies, with *Sky One* on.
One guest had a mullet; a fatty beaver's pelt, cap-kinked.
His girlfriend had asked him onto *Springer* to propose:
her lips an arse in pink PVC,
roots blackening her perm in a partial eclipse.
Her heft squidged from Lycra, like mince from a taco –
'I love you babe, I want you to be mah husband.'

The eyes of others solidify our sense of self –
hence there, then, that woman with her showboat slow voice
risked whispers at the fried chicken joint
for one faltering moment in the world's indifferent glare.
He said no –
no to Vegas, and babies, and love.
In came the obligatory transsexual rival,
then the cat-spat, the tribe's chant: 'Go Jerry! Go Jerry!'
Two tuna-pasta-gobbling bodyguards tugged them apart.
The televised close-up of a shattering heart.
'You just trash honey, mah man aint marrying no ho' like you.'

My mum supped on her brew,
and in my lap was half a poem addressed to the boy
I never told I loved or hated, until he read it in print.
A confession: I enjoyed that TV show.
A confession: mine was a selfish art, and desperate; I wanted *you*
        to care.

Madder

All my sins are mortal
CARAVAGGIO

Low clouds expand upwards through a scalding storm sky,
a torched brown; like smoky, perfumed tea from the orient
pushing against boiled water's rolling plunge.
At *Palazzo Madama*, in Rome – my beloved *Roma* –
patrons sipped teas such as these, feet snug on eastern rugs.
They drank fine wines, velvet as sooty blood,
that lay, endlessly corked, in the earth's dark.
Not for me such acts of patient preservation: I'd have supped
the bacchic juices straight away; their crimsons calling for it.
I cannot forgo fists of juicing grapes for the promise
of a future sip of papal wine, when the final mass comes.

The clouds are raw sienna, bumps to windfall fruit,
a shaft of light's strike through a young boy's nut-brown hair.
This storm may mean to scour Naples of sinners –
the thieving *lazzaroi* who flick up mucky soles,
date-plump whores; the feverish, jeering crowd by the gallows,
the gypsies, dicers, drinkers, and – I know – myself,
perhaps the mortal who has sinned the most.
Michel Angelo Caravaggio, murderer – slathered
in our inner vermilion. Red, red always my colour.
Once Rome was at my soiled feet, now I picture its domes –
by the storm's spilt light – as bright, cold shoulders.

You recognise my face? It's true, I've gathered fame –
and who could forget a face such as this –
the massy fringe of black, brows thick as infidel's fingers,
hooded eyes – fat and jellied as eggs – their irises
shining dark coals, strong olives, sucked grapes?
It is a face that hints at stabbings, screwings, rapes.
You may have seen a self-portrait: *The Sick Bacchus*
or *The Taking of Christ*, where primed-canvas pale bones
were draped in my own swarthy, bestial form,
and true to form, forgive me Christ for I have sinned,
in the Taverns of the Turk, the Blackamoor and the Wolf,

and I do not regret my sins: not one night
of gambling gems and scudi on a heart-beat's luck,
not one trip to the banks of the Tiber, the *Ortaccio* –
our own garden of evil – for a sperm-clotted cunt,
not one hot, sweet boy with a dimpled heart-face
puffing on his delicate lute, or heaped with armfuls of fruit
who has flushed from the eyes to the chin
at my slow, florid plunge. Not one rash draw
of the sword, or the knife, in evening's half-light –
the scrabble, and jolt, and the man folding in on himself –
or stone thrown at the window of a poor whore.

No, if I had not been exiled from Rome – beloved *Roma* –
I would not regret. Though I have tried to be godly
it's life, every time, that bludgeons my skull, wanting in.
And life's bound to flesh, that is selfish and needy of sin,
that craves oranges against a cyan sky, to be wooed
by the madrigal, mirrors, a courtesan's mouth –
its beauty spot a full stop by the spent cock – vengeance
felt in the straightening of an elbow, and cold.
Life, that is carmine, ruby, russet, scarlet, cardinal –
that is every shade of red from perfect love, to pain, to carnal.
That demands that it be lived, not just preserved.

My *Boy Bitten by a Lizard* tells a truth – reach out to life,
and pain may cause your hand to spasm to a claw.
Ugliness and agony are what we pay to be made flesh –
even Mary's nails were spades, and her belly distended –
and they cry out at my Christ's scuffed heels! He was made man
with all the degradation that brings, and I could love him
only like this: tempted, torn and weak, and wearing red.
You heard about the *banda capitale*? Well each of us
has a death sentence on our head, and it could strike at any time,
in any place, like a storm's fevered race towards our sky.
The red of blood is spilt out living, not the death you die.

Adventures with Lola

1 *With Lola in Paris*

Lola has a Nefertiti fringe,
and eyes cut from onyx.
She holds a flame up to the sugar-spoon –
concentrating –
a child with a chemistry kit.

This morning we drank black coffee on the Left Bank,
her voice crackly as old jazz:
'You just don't get me, sweet, I'm fucked up.'
I bought her white tulips,
bloodless mouths puckered for kisses,

but now she's hearing voices, stealing babies,
smashing up the bar, moaning: 'Help me'.
There are cuts on her cocaine-pale arms.

I hold her at night, carefully:
her head's a cuckoo's egg, her body porn.

2 *With Lola in New York*

Lola wears all black.
She's been living on pretzels.
The skyline's a block full of knives
that, from Brooklyn bridge, she reaches out towards,
her body arched, a street-lamp, over the railing.

'So we fucked all night,' she gloats.
'He tied me to the bed, he made me beg.'
Yesterday we stole masks from a thrift shop –
hers a cat's –
and I bought her cocktails, sweet as pop,
until the chink of a tip caught her gold-digger's ears.

She shows me a ring, from Tiffany's,
the jewel big as a Belgian chocolate.
'Shall I jump?' she asks. 'Fuck you, I want to jump.'

3 *With Lola in Berlin*

Lola's hair is bleached Dietrich blonde,
a chandelier of light.
The smoky bar bristles
like a cat sensing the presence of a ghost
as she enters stage-left
and shooby-dos to me, at the back.

At her request, I am wearing a suit –
dark and slim as liquorice –
and my hair slicked back.

Afterwards, there's whisky, prairie oysters,
we shuffle a slow-dance, swaying like our images in water.
'Hau ab,' she tells approaching boys,
hardening her chafed vowels to gunshot.

Down the Kurfurstendamm
she says: 'Just fucking kiss me.'
In my arms she is perfume, and pain.
Here, now – in the street? 'Yes.'

My Bed

Tracy Emin lives down the road from me,
and recently's had notable acclaim
due to a certain bed. As poetry's
in need of press, I thought I'd do the same –
show you the place I slept and dreamt and came!
Admittedly, it's not in the best taste,
but self-promotion must be *in-yer-face*.

The bed's not strictly mine, more my boyfriend's,
given him by his sister, which was nice.
It's broken, but it's okay for our ends –
insomnia's a poet's favourite vice.
So now the guided tour – just some advice –
don't sniff too deep, I haven't washed the sheets
for weeks, and there may be a tang of yeast.

Here is the pillow where my sleepy head
has left an indent, like a world war bomb.
Here's the wet patch, and here is where I said:
'If you're getting a drink please get me one,'
the snot that I fished out when he was gone,
and sneaked under the valance; the mishap
where I splodged gravy, eating off my lap.

Here is the duvet, under which I sweat
through many a long, dark night of the heart,
where I wrote 'Knowledge', 'Post', and other hits,
the dark and foetal hothouse of my art.
Where bedbugs gnaw my flesh, and cut skin starts
to be repaired. It's here I get whiny
when it seems football's always on TV.

Not intimate enough? Here's a cum-rag
that's fallen down the side and not been seen –
observe its crisp petals and grubby clag.
Imagine I am wiping myself clean!
And from the tissue box feel free to glean
that I am more concerned with cash than flash –
they are Economy; rough as a rash.

Is this too explicit for you to take?
Unlikely, when *Big Brother*'s a success,
stardom fingered Airplane's Jeremy Spake,
and Trisha has them queuing to confess.
Everyone loves to prod a stranger's mess,
so come prod mine, it's English literature!
Decide if it's postmodern, or just 'raw'.

Of course, I am a serious artist –
to whom, in future, critics will defer –
so though it's true I'm always on the piss,
it does not mean my art does not refer.
I hope 'My Bed' will be able to stir
memories of bed-tricks on Renaissance stage,
of Donne's flea-ridden bed; Othello's rage,

and *À la recherche du temps perdu*
Proust wrote, of course, in bed, whilst ill and glum.
The irony that I'm addressing you
laid out in the same fashion, with numb bum,
remembrance conjured not by bun, but crumb,
I do hope is not lost, though I can't bank
on readers looking past the sex and wank.

The bed has always been a potent spot.
The site of birth and death, as well as verse.
For most of us, sex takes place there a lot,
and rarely in anywhere more perverse.
It's where we vomit, sip soup and are nursed.
It's where we construct plans, fondle our fears;
go for a spin after too many beers.

The bed's the seething breeding ground of life –
our one escape; the prop that drags us back.
The place where we are our real, beastly selves,
and yet in which were most likely to act.
At night, in bed, reality's attacked –
were forced to relive what we can't undo,
and all's a shifting blur of false and true.

And as for 'My Bed', well, I'm fond of it,
sleep on the left, and as a lanky bitch
am far too long to be a proper fit.
Its bacteria induce the odd itch,
but still, I'm in no hurry for a switch.
Let's face it, Saatchi's unlikely to buy –
although I'm listening if he wants to try.

It hasn't been the craziest of beds,
you'd find as interesting all about –
just as I've not the most exciting head,
only some massive need to write things out.
If 'My Bed' has a message, it's to shout:
all life's potential art, all that is real
interests people – hence docusoap's appeal.

What a resonant and rich life we lead
when Darren feeding chickens in real-time's
enough to keep the nation hooked with need
to know what happened next, when parking crimes
have their own show, and artists in their prime
can turn the entire art world on its head
with one explicit, splendid, loaded bed!

Puppetry

It comes quietly, is something spilt,
a cup of tea nudged over whilst I slept;
a leakage of silence that weeps through sludge
my skull cups like a preciousness.

It is the chemicals, my doctor says:
they puppet me, softly drip from my mind
to soak through muscle's petticoats; the heart's damp walls.
A silt of hurt is backing up my veins.

To wake to this, in this crotch-scented bed,
this skin, a *day*, is fear. I watch my strings –
translucent tendons – web the wobbling air
above my slump, and who in hell will pull?

It is an effort, to lift up the foot,
one knee, a thigh; to sway in my sad sweat.
In the kitchen, a voice thrown onto me
squeaks: *yes, of course, oh, just had a big night,*

and I pop pills from pharmacies and hippies.
So many puppeteers! They slug it out.
The wind's a wolf; the sun its greasy eye.
No, none of that, this is not imagery...

it is not tea, or puppetry, or beasts,
this is me sniping snide remarks at you
for no reason, and you saying: you're twisted,
and walking out with a frown like real life.

I wash up, staring out at next door's kid,
her dolls, and think on death, but I soon scare
that it is just like this. Things bleed.
I think, no, *know*, my soul is not my soul.

Posing for Dante Gabriel Rossetti

So, look at me one last time:
paint the hair hanging in plush red curtains
around the show of my face,

skin titanium white,
hips sharp as bent paint tubes.
Would you like to take me – in my thick laudanum trance –

my hair splattering the pillows like coughed-up blood
as you sign your name on a corner of me?
Sometimes we play dress-up –

out come the robes, the archaisms – *sire* –
and I'm Beatrice or – *Be Ophelia*, you plead,
and I heed, and am still as a moat.

Three hours I've been still –
the tapestry grates at my nipples,
faintness swamps my head,

I am drowning in a bath of pins;
leaden-skirted, dead-legged.
You say: *Poor lovely Lizzie, you've a poetic soul* –

but I try, and each poem's ABAB,
each weak pencil line is still-born
like our child smeared in oils:

violet, cobalt, chalk.
It's face was a picture erased – paper-pale,
and inscribed with indents of loss...

Time to pass me the opiates over, I think.
As you watch my blotting-paper eyes soak up ink,
please know that I'm circling hell, and hell's who I am,

and who I am's whoever you want me to be,
which is no one.
And yes, I will move my arm.

A Winter's Tale

Snow creaks on firs;
the sky is water on paper.
Fragile with shopping, I shuffle
from the shops, each step struggling to soar.

The house is comparatively warmer.
By the radiator I am Hermione,
thaw weeping through my stone body,
heat's crawl bloodying my fingers.
A word, perhaps, and this carved lip would tremble.
A touch, and my veins might bear their blood...

No. The drifts of my skin (immaculate
as snow, you said) are now frost on glass:
shattered with lines, bitter.
We cannot see each other for it.

I remind myself you love that girl, scarcely older
than our lost daughter should have been now,
had she not cooled in her crib.

You are eating your smackerel of something, gob clacking
on mushed bread, your tongue damply balling.
Later, your tongue will frisk to the taste
of sinuous meat, the tug
of its silvery threads: a breaking of flesh.

Do you awaken her slim fingers briskly
between rasping hands?
Before she touches your burning body
does she raise her hands to her mouth
to steam the tent of them?

Inside the house is dark.
Outside is a blinding carpet of light,
which my clumsy feet would snuff grey.
Sixteen winters now I have been a statue,
waiting for redemption, recovery.
Wondering by what magic
your hot hand on my cool cheek would not burn.

The Black Widow

Slug-trails of spittle clotted his old mouth,
the dry, black moth of it.
His fingers burrowed into my flesh,
like blind worms, finding death in me.
Coveting youth, he would clamp on my neck,
drinking it in, growing swollen with blood.

His tastes were conventional:
a black, leather mini-skirt that made my butt look
like two cockroaches mating.
Lashes like spider legs, and a mouth
fat and red as a mosquito bite gone bad.
One night I pounded powder up and slipped it in his drink.

It fell on his heart like a tempest of furious bees;
his heart battered in his chest like a bee in a jar.
Luring him into my parlour, to the lace of my bed,
I writhed on him until he was dead.
Now I still wear black, but only finest silk,
and people spin unsubstantiated truths;

hoard their rumours and clues, not knowing
how my life has been a fluttering towards light,
then glass's smack, or else singed wings.
How the secrets my father laid in my flesh
like flies' eggs, hatched to maggots,
and hollowed my chest clean out.

Doubter's Sonnets

I

And if there is a God, and he is good –
as we presume – then how come all the pain?
Why is it so taboo to help the good?
Why give the appetites of rats free rein?
Why let plagues rage; children stop in their cots,
and pose for porn, and accidentally drown;
and people starve, and scream to the black box,
and smash, and contract AIDS, and get so down

about this godless fucked-up earth he gave
that it unpicks their hearts and makes souls dead –
and let the cordial of his sweet gifts
corrode us, for something that he's not said.
So he wants faith / free-will / must use his rod?
There is no God. I could not forgive God.

II

And if there is a God, why is he good?
Why so presume, when there's no evidence?
A person who is all your world may die
tomorrow, with no reason or defence,
and when their coffin cracks, and lilies droop
and drip – their stamen and their chlorophyll
evidence of the Greater Plan, some claim –
singeing to gloop, then ash, talk of God's will

or heaven will not reassure at all,
as heaven's not for frailties or for touch,
or sweaty palms, or angry fits, or scars,
or other human things we love so much.
They say that Jesus died to save us all –
yet still we're damned; still comes the sickly fall.

III

But hold on, am I being too PC –
A left wing, liberal drip, a bleeding heart –
presuming that I'm on the side of right,
while he is not, who was at starting's start?
Now individuality's a cult,
and each of us presume joy is our right,
God may think we need seasoning in grief –
showing the self's also a thing to fight.

Perhaps he speaks, but I refuse to hear –
once proof was tablets, prophets, locusts, nails;
now scientists find his hand in the lungs,
star-punctuated skies, and shell-cupped snails.
As God wrote down his words in stone, not sand,
perhaps it's unfair – wanting a re-brand.

IV

Please God, batter my heart, and make me feel
a fervour in the place of this huge lack!
But who am I talking to anyway?
A childhood certainty that I want back,
no more. No really, face it, there's nothing
except the brain, nature's chemistry kit –
no benevolent old guy in the sky
or devil tempting us to use our bits;

no Jesus with his wound a velvet purse,
to plunge hands in and pull redemption out –
no water turning to a Chardonnay,
or anything, to stem sensible doubt.
Let's dwell a second – adults – on the facts:
the harmless crap, these self-deluding acts.

V

If you would please ignore my arguments,
I would be glad – my lack of faith depletes.
It can't bring paper petals to seal love,
or conjure song, or bake fat cakes to eat.
It makes impossible a loved, lost hand;
brings no fresh starts, just fleshy, messy ends.
Fuck staring truth and death straight in the face –
I don't recommend godlessness to friends.

Here hopelessness grows until the past groans,
and there's no comfort in a future 'when',
only that vista of beloved things
and people we may never touch again.
We've so much *more* to us – we should transcend –
but no, we're here, we die and we pretend.

Bed Scenes

1 *Sleep-Talking*

cold rain sizzles on the pane
my eyes begin to decode darkness
my husband's thick-ribbed back is a hulking fist, they'd had fun
he said
he'd bought her sweets to shut her up – her mouth was a split fig,
     the house
was a doll's house my husband,
                          my husband placed on the sofa
before the wrong TV show (Ready Steady Cook they made a
     golden pear tart)
my daughter neatly put in a bath she didn't need

both moved by some sudden, giant hand

there is a rat downstairs, it scuttles behind the washer
heavy and larded, its eyes beads of sweat
my daughter, my daughter it is chewing now
in all our secret places
street light tongues wetly through the crack
                        between curtains

rain splutters on the pane like fingers dunked
in spittle, his buried fingers

I feign sleep

night breathes on our beaded bodies through the flung-
open window, sweat cool on me like myrrh
my heart racing like the hunted

are we not blessed with this violet this banging moon
which strikes our skins silver
tangles pale fingers in our hair?

you hold me tight
                      such a passion, the heavy-scented
stocks faint music an alarm going off
and the grasses drawing fluid to themselves
                                   touch turns liquid
rising in my throat a cry
                     no stopping this the pounding
of my heart the tightening the breaking

and me all whole beneath the weight of you

And Desire Shall Fail

The belly sickens, but the heart is never full,
because there are a thousand mouths inside our blood.
You cannot fight this needy drag; the self's old pull.

Even champagne when it's attained can become dull –
every desire, when it's fulfilled, becomes a dud.
The belly sickens, but the heart is never full.

What we demand – more things, more love – is pitiful.
Though we are well-off, healthy, sheltered, understood –
we do not fight this needy drag; the self's old pull.

And though sometimes romance can briefly pull the wool,
temptation brings us back to ourselves with a thud.
The belly sickens, but the heart is never full.

The heart's a tyrant that won't tolerate a lull.
Look at our luck: no war, no famine and no flood,
yet there's no one who can resist the self's old pull.

There's no *enough* that enough days cannot annul,
and though you may be kind, and liberal, and good,
you will not fight this needy drag; the self's old pull.
The belly sickens, but the heart is never full.

Fantasy Dinner Party

To the soft blue scales of Miles Davis, my cocktail shaker
gargles vodka martinis, that harden to diamonds in their glasses,
olives caught in their wet mouths like flies.

Then I lead my guests to the table – its bowls of origami-crisp lilies,
the bright croci of my candle flames. Champagne fizzles
up my nose when Dorothy Parker delivers a one-liner,
but then she observes that champagne doesn't go with *pâté de foie gras*,
and John Lennon says *pâté de foie gras* is cruel, and – I quote –
Instant Karma's gonna get me.

I hurry out the main course.
The quails stewed in their own juices are a reasonable success,
although not macrobiotic enough for John, apparently,
who is harping on about having no possessions
like the song hasn't been released three times.
Frank O'Hara confesses he's a shopoholic, John mutters poof,
and Germaine Greer calls John repressed, which is probably true,
but I'm not having one of the Beatles coming out at my dinner
              party...

So I attempt to change the mood by saying: Sylvia –
how about a poem?
                    You can guess the rest.
Walter Benjamin is not all that impressed with her: '*I may
be a bit of a Jew*' line, and she starts sobbing into those big gold bangs,
and gets a moustache of snot,
and virtually tells us Ted was impossible, although
we've all read *The Birthday Letters* now,
                              and don't know what to believe.

The dessert, a bloated, dribbling summer pudding from M & S
has pulped to a smashed skull in its box,
and everyone's polite, but suddenly Frank has to go to the 5-Spot,
and Dorothy to the Algonquin,
                    and the others spill out of the door.
Their heads push down into the wetness, frowning.

In the kitchen, amongst scraps of contaminated tuna, mashed livers,
slop, and pans brimming with cold water, I weep
because I wasn't
                    good enough, and they were not
as good as we need them to be,
and because it rained tonight of all nights.

Richard, my boyfriend, says don't worry –
I'll do the washing up, go to bed.

Knowing Our Limits

Cough-racked, my lungs crunched brittle air,
my bark-lined neck dripped sap,
and you, awoken by my chest's clutching,
its rough, buried explosions, pressed a kiss

on my damp forehead, laughed to hear
my nasal bubblings; the jellied nose and lungs.
Outside the city's light-washed sky
was starless, but my jarred body grew

to remember its place in the scale. My cold
was common. You brought me tea, saying:
warmth can cure by slackening the throat,
but of course, some things cannot be cured,

and my bone-cage still rattled all night –
just as we can never be enough
for each other, or keep back the frost-stung air,
but can help, which is plenty.

Letter from a Father

My wife – comic already, see,
that *my* must have raised a chortle –
you look at me and see a balding clown:
cross eyes, a glacé cherry nose,
my mouth blubbery white, a peeled banana,
my penis a banana skin.
I'm a joke for you and your girlfriends
(sorry *women*-friends – slapped wrists!)
a gnome, sent to smoke in the garden;
a goblin grotesquery gobbling
tinned hot-dog sandwiches, meat pie, peas –
man's food –
                    passé, outré –
a gargoyle at the window, waiting for you to come home.

Of course, I had my tired *I want to be*'s –
at five, a fireman, at twelve, cricket (a bowler) for Lancashire –
but they wintered to clichéd *not to be*'s,
and instead I settled for mundane masculinity –
working hard for that conservatory,
anniversary in Paris, second mortgage, respect.
You gave me a tit-wank sometimes:
you made the boys packed lunches whilst
I taught them to play chess.

Then you began to waft off my advances, like farts,
later, laughed them off altogether.
Seemed I'd turned into some sad flasher in the park,
a bearded-lady.

We downsized to a Fiesta.
Lager on my breath meant separate beds –
I could not deign to touch you in your dignity, maturity,
to touch that *Special K* figure.
Your hair lacquered to a helmet,
your face plastered to a mask.
You were brisk, efficient, immaculate
with your *Next* suits, your *River Café* cookbook,
your promotion, your nail extensions, lunching with friends,

and my dead ends,
and my cock, some dumb, aquatic feeler –
a visual gag –
                    I was a slapstick slaphead!

Slid down the evolutionary ladder,
from man to monkey; Rambo to Dumbo.
Other men find solace in drink –
but whisky morphed me in your glare
to a rosy-cheeked leprechaun;
beer made me Homer Simpson, gargling Duff, belching,
slapping my head – *D'oh!*

I wanked into a tissue. Shag McNasty
said 'Worship the cock'. That girl did not laugh.

Once I was the chairman of the PTA
(sorry, chair*person* – slapped wrists!)
There's no such thing as masculinism.
No future for a man in this queered world
of pine-nuts, Girl Power, 'relationships',

and you said I'm having the kids,
no question; that's a mother's rights,
the law, hands down, and I said
you're not having my sons I love them too,
and you said: who carried them, suckled them,
cleaned their little bums, did the school run?

but I could take them and I took them.
I didn't like Andrew seeing,
but I could only do one at a time.
To you I'm like that dog with sunshades and a cigar
that you got snapped with in Marbella;
but you won't laugh when you read now
how I wanted them with me, safe
from dole queues, bitches, date-rape,
litigation off the woman at work that you ask to make tea,
all that giggling over Chardonnay,
                                shame.
you said you'd change their name –

you said I'd never see my lovely boys.
Death is a man, he will give me my dignity.
God is a man, and a father, and will understand.

On Tragic Pleasure

Another train crash has arranged itself over grass –
a shattered spine, a bludgeoned serpent.
A mobile phone rings – to the tune of a-ha's 'Take on Me' –
from its dark guts,
                    ceasing at the switch to answer-phone:
I'm sorry I'm not here at the moment...

Dionysus is here, crouched, bullish in near fields,
black grapes draped slack around his throat;
                                           a little drunk.
As they try to cut a girl from the train's fist,
it is he who cuts our pain
                    with pleasure, to: *temper and reduce*
to just measure with a kind of sweetness

so that huddled round the water-cooler, waiting for new news to break,
there's a sweet frisson;
the messenger who brings the death-toll spins the detail out,
a tease,
         excitement's tremor barely checked.

Dust thickens like off-milk;
                    the search slows,
it's on the front page of the *Metro*.
'Wasn't it a tragedy?' The till-girl asks –
'Fourteen dead, possibly five more.'

We are punished far in excess of our guilt.

And news churns all day:
'no details yet but our world exclusive footage shows
torn metal, where gummy flesh displays itself –
an advert for chops or for child abuse –
its snaky tubes and unfathomable blood webs...'

From beginnings we loved tragedy –
to sit on sun-warm stone, the *sssh* of wind in olive-trees,
and masked corpses drying out in the heat like figs.
To witness death

                              distantly.
To know it yet know that it won't touch us.

Our sense of horror falters with *hard use* –
dogs find the seams of foxes; bulls' innards splash –
like badly served rhubarb crumble in school canteen –
on sawdust; cock fights cock, crowds whoop.

Now there's telly –
                              we learn to crave the thrill of flying punches;
a man's mushed head spitting off a squall of sweat
as the mat thumps up, and its 10-9-8-
                              'Come on, Rocky!'
-4-3-2-
          and 'Rocky Balboa is champion of the world!'

But whilst the Greeks witnessed death without masks
and skene, our dying are driven
                              to *Casualty* or *ER*.
And real death is in the fake's same frame –
not Palestine again,
                    turn over, love –

so a crisis – it's a buzz! – it's something –
it's a taste of TV, TV becoming life, and suddenly
you're *in* TV, you're a camera, and suffering, well,
suffering's entertainment, that's all –

until you fall, and your mind's struck to madness,
and you're taking gulps of *no, no, no, no, no,*

and people are staring at your flickering face.

Work and Lunch

He goes to Prêt-à-Manger every day,
likes something chickeny, or maybe Thai,
takes it back to the office to bolt, an e-mail dinner,
or perhaps – if, like today, he has a window –
to this sunstruck square of grass
that is alive with suits, WAP phones and knees,
crammed as a slave-ship, or the *Mayflower*,
to broil his nose and ankles FT pink.

Sunspot screensavers burn into his eyes,
and he notes a growth in interest, as the temp from accounts
hitches her skirt up, chopsticking
thick coins of sushi into her parched mouth.
A pigeon pecking at the prematurely balding grass
finds the nub of a Cajun tortilla wrap,
a frill of lollo rosso, then flaps up to settle
on one roof along the square's concrete sales graph.

The May sky is cloudless, and as azure
as Stephenson's head on the five pound note.
Summer means smart-casual, so he wears chinos,
is porcine in a *Paul Smith* shirt – its cost a mere drop
out of fifty grand a year, plus bonuses.
Dinner, later, could be the cracked cymbals of poppadoms,
the thick-lipped gob of a burger,
the bloated water lilies of prawn crackers.

And fifty grand a year, plus bonuses,
is pretty fair, he thinks, when all's accounted for –
the nine-to-nine, the bolted bagels, RSI,
and these inadequate and sandwiched blasts of sun,
this child's cress-patch of grass,
the numbness of the arse,
the tube train where he stands, jammed,
correspondence in a filing cabinet.

His half hour up, he stands and sweeps
his trousers clear of blades with heat-damp hands.
These gobbled-down breaks will soon be a rarity
if – fingers crossed – he gets his rise: such work demands.
A black girl picks up empty cans with pincers,
and John, who is on sixty-five, has sent a text:
ptcher + piano ltr? it asks. *Yes*, he begins to reply,
then, thinking twice, sends simply *y*.

Post-

Let me describe what I am seeing: the trees fracture
the skyline like cracks, the sun's a peeled egg –
then a steel-wool sky, and fields like carpet tiles.
You know the scene: think Roman Polanski's *Tess*
or a gentleman's horse-heightened view in an Austen adaptation.
It's been described before: the trees as hands, the sun a coin,
the sky slate, the fields patchwork, probably.
And my new words don't serve it any better – let's face it,

are unlikely even to be new, now novelty's no novelty.
So why do we poets keep cranking it out: love, death,
lovers, mothers, nature – all of hackneyed humanity?
Hannah tells me this pessimism's arrogance, assuming that
because we cannot forge newness ourselves then no one can.
The Greeks once mourned the same – their future's absence.
But then there was a world to find – now all's been mapped,
branded, sampled, split. Iceland's a tourist trap;

this England sprawled before me belongs to the past.
Think of it as arriving at a party where the drink's drunk,
the cheese is chalky ruins, and some pisshead
is slurring out his theory about the point of life –
as though you hadn't heard it all before. These trees
are Plath's *black fingers*, Keats bagged the *maturing sun*,
and each field's filtered through a thousand Emmerdales. Look,
the sky is *darkening like a stain*. We are too late, anyway.

The Florist's

After a dark rattling through dark places –
through earth packed tight against my entrance –
stumbling up into the tube station's decayed mouth
to wait for my date, I see a florist's, startling
as a corsage tacked onto an old shirt used for painting.
There are freesias like wet fingerprints,
gerberas like parrot-eyes.
Pink rosebuds are the slippery heads of newborn mice;
arum lilies seem the sun-bleached skulls of cattle;
carnations used tissues strewn
in the wake of a bad flu.

There is a preacher loitering too – thick bearded, crazy-eyed –
who booms at me, Moses with a loudspeaker:
Open your eyes to God,
who designed the intricate wonders of these blooms, as he made you,
and you will die as flowers do.
Before it is too late, open up your eyes.
He has picked the wrong atheist, and only leads my thoughts
to how these flowers are snapped –
suspended briefly in their own pure thirst –
their certain, rapid deaths mapped out; soon for the bin.
They have no souls to race up to meet God,
and nor do we.

But still, as beside this believer I gaze
on the faint stars of narcissi;
on the wine-glass heads of tulips, full of Merlot;
on the gypsophilia, like a cow's frozen breath –
a sense of blessedness makes me tell him:
Though I see no greater hand, please do not think
this astounding beauty wasted for one moment upon me.

Morning

This aching is all
that I trust not to leave –
whilst my wine-crusted tongue
makes other lovers heave,

this one kisses me full,
sinks affectionate hands
down into the cores
of my bones; my plans.

Once there were reasons –
I'd wake and locate,
here, cruelty's cut,
here, a hole gouged by hate,

or betrayal his mouth
had stubbed out on my cheek.
Now I am my own reason –
self-pitying, weak –

for this body won't heal,
and this bright skin draws dirt.
My incompetent heart
haemorrhages hurt.

Gender Wars

He's such a *man*, she says, spittingly –
snacking on rolling news, then reeling off death-names,
detailing how daisy-cutters scorch a six hundred-yard radius.
She's leaving her husband with the baby and B-52s
whilst we go out to *Pizza Express* for girlish natter,
and doughballs wallowing fatly in butter,
one cheesecake, two spoons.
'If women ran things,' she crows,
checking her bag for her mobile with fingertips florid with rouge,
all damp coat and perfume, fussing:
'there would be no war.'

And as her fingers race over slick teak, to the lamp's pad-dulled
          switch,
I imagine Ilse Koch's fingers performing the same gesture,
her hands crunchy with diamonds,
and the lightshade of tattooed skin that her husband
procured her from Auschwitz losing its light –
ships and butterflies plunged to a darkness.
Wonder whether she could not help but lift up
a finger to touch on that softest hide, its each inked stitch a hurt;
the thrilling warmth of it.

Oistros

My daughter, I fed you with beef –
with spag bol, burgers, shepherd's pie –
and now, my love, you have to die,
for I did feed you up with grief.

Too many times I fed you crap –
It is Medea, turned to farce!
When proper cooking seemed an arse,
I'd warm up junk-food, frozen pap.

But what I did I did not know.
Like gods, the politicians pleased
to lead me into ironies –
they did not teach me to say no,

and now your mind's begun to drift.
I cut my cooking time by half –
it's made you falter like a calf;
my daughter, fallen for their thrift.

To Undefine

As this train races over dull rungs, northwards,
to 'home', or what I still slip to call that,
air is whetted, fields tense with the faint burden of frost,
and autumn's honed to picture-book precision.
Distancing myself from adulthood's warm, louche season –
how London's trees still slosh with green
long after they have wept their Christmas lights –
my head is full of *then*:
the shoals of red and umber leaves,
tar-clammy toffees swaddled up in greaseproof squares,
the gluts of conkers I would shell with heels,
and with my father, his hand mittening mine.

But that was before I began to unlearn things I knew –
the blueness of the sea, the 'evil' of Iraq and – my mother
claimed – red wine.
Before the bonfire where they placed a slant, grey fence, to keep
me back
from poking twigs and chair-legs onto flame,
and other men, whose 'love' meant something shifting, dark.
We curve near lawns shag-piled by mowers put away too early,
and slow for Piccadilly,
where my mother's small, hot body stands sprung
to launch fretfully on mine – half-child, half-her's.
Later, with my father, I'll mash leaves with tread
to make out where – give or take – we saw the owl.
The fallen tree that may have been my den.

And Another Bloody Thing...
(after Wendy Cope)

Bloody men are like bloody cigarettes –
A habit you swear you'll crack,
Then you find you've snuck out of the office
To suck one off round the back.